Apple Trash, Blood Clouds, and Seeds

Acho 61* Books
1419 Heathrow Court
Milford OH 45150
Acho61@mail.com

ISBN: 978-1-105-43613-0

Foreword

To know Jack Dolezal is to know his faith, family and friends.

He is passionate about these things and, in turn, it shows through his poetry.

A man in pursuit of God, doing his honest best to: raise his children in

God's love while being a Godly example; love his wife as Christ loves the

church; be the best friend he can possibly be while being the best imitator of

Christ. Does he do all of these perfectly? No, but he is not

afraid to try or to share his successful or failed attempts.

One of the many reasons he and I are friends.

Many of the poems you are about to encounter will be based on the above,

Jack sharing his life with you and his sharing of life experiences with others.

Others will come from the additional joys in his life – music and sports and

some other odds and ends. How does a man with a wife and five children to

care for and all the other busy-ness of life find the time or energy

to write of his life experiences much less remember them?

However it is done I am glad that he does it.

Jack, I count it a privilege to be your friend and am honored to write this

foreword. In your poem Chimmy you write "I have to be the best me, I

would be a lousy someone else". Thank you for

being the best you and encouraging me to be the best me.

Sharing life with you has been a blessing.

YBIC

Bret Leveline

You Do Not Deserve Me

An exquisite control of emotion
Love, the only I see
Physically, emotionally, and intellectually stimulating
You say you do not deserve me

You shed a tear when I voiced my emotions
Saying with you, I wish to be
You said you think you were always in love
You say you do not deserve me

You love my family and my friends
Occasionally it is you they would rather see
Giving gifts, caring, and listening
You say you do not deserve me

You are correct, Patricia, you do not deserve me
We both are aware of this fact
You deserve one million times better
Because of this, He and I have a pact

I cannot love someone out of my league
With you, this is the case
Only through Him should you get what you deserve
And in me, you shall see His face

If I achieve one percent of my intentions
Your heart will truly rejoice
For I am fortunate to receive the privilege
To, "Love Patty!", said His voice

Inspiration: Patty lovingly told me she did not feel like she
deserved me. This is my way of agreeing with her, and as I said,
she deserves much, much better.

Chimmy

I want to see you in all things I experience
But I just do not want the feeling of my childhood church
I love getting to know you through movies, radio, and nature
Not only through the acceptable Christian safe search

It is all yours and we do not always remember that
Some run in fear on certain days
You are with me at all times and in all situations
I can run boldly in the dark, You are the way

I have to be the best me, I would be a lousy someone else
Their ways are theirs and it is You in them that attracts
It is You in me that the light shines brightest in obedience
When I attempt anything else is when I lack

Inspiration: Meeting with others I am inspired by spiritually but different than I
am, makes me want to be like them. God reminds me they are bright because they
are being what He created them and them only to be. When I am being what He
created me to be, I am at my peak and that is what He wants for all of us.

Who Am I

They said goodbye to him today
Children are not supposed to go before parents
Their hearts in more pieces than a shattered crystal glass
Devastation on this day had no fence

They shook hands with those who came
The rain outside was the right backdrop
So many cried, we grieved as one
Yet their loss will be a forever pain throb

They believe so they knew there will be a reunion soon
That thought is a balm on their heartache
They say goodbye to friends and him on this day
Their lives and plans without him begin to be made

Inspiration: My friends lost their son a couple years ago. This is dedicated to him
and them.

Rainbow

We walk on the opposite side of the tracks
Though our friendship is strong
We share many of the same interests
The tenure of our relationship has been long

Alike in so many ways except one
Still enjoy the company
Your humor, intelligence, and kind heart
Your cast of admirers, many

So many similarities on your side and mine
Yet they will always be separate
We still talk and connect
Neither of us have any regrets

I am glad to know you
Sometimes I want to tell people to relax
We look and speak the same
We walk on the opposite side of the tracks

Inspiration: I have many gay friends, this is written for them.

Her

You just changed my life
Your presence lifted my spirit
In all the pain that surrounds me, it leaves for a moment
I have no debt

It is all going to be ok
No one needs to tell me
I know because of you in my life
The sun shines through you I see

Just smile once again
It helps me through the day
I can go on because of you
And it is from nothing you say

Inspiration: My wife Patty walking in the room.

Fairytale

I think about our first Christmas
We took so many pictures
Nothing would stop the joy of this time
In our community, our family would be fixtures

We did not have anything
No money to buy each other presents
Just seeing your face by candlelight at night
Tomorrow I will worry about the rent

So many years have passed
I do not even know where you are now
What began so amazingly and ended so badly
I go through my memories and ask, how?

That water flowed under the bridge so long ago
More whiskey flows down my throat
I am still saying goodbye, you just do not know it
A lifetime ago you told me that was all she wrote

Inspiration: Loosely inspired by The Pogues with
Kirsty MacColl classic Christmas tune, "Fairytale
of New York"

England

You woke me up in my waking season
I loved the accent and guitar
Still wearing my Beatle boots and gelling my hair
Music had become an important part

Saying goodbye to her in my own way
Saying hello to school for the first time
Saying I do not care for the things I used to
Saying the truth instead of just a line

Now twenty-five years later you are still playing
I am pretending to be an adult
Your music is digital and being tubed by you
Yet that day your prose was, of my earth, the salt

Inspiration: Heard the song by Billy Bragg "A New England" in 1985 one morning on
the radio while listening to my favorite station, WOXY and had not heard it since and did
not even know the name. I instantly loved it. I came across it twenty-five years later

Cupid

The day of love
Countless emotions experienced by so many
I remember breaking up with a girlfriend on this day
I remember my wife beginning our relationship in plenty

Some so bitter at what they do not have
Others so consumed with what they receive
Young, old, male, female all do it differently
Just do not tell me you do not believe

I loved showing my girlfriends and now my spouse
With as large of plans that I could financially create
To woo them and publically declare my feelings for them
Oftentimes jealous coworkers it makes

I absolutely love Valentines Day
I love going over the top for my wife
I am committed to show her not only in a twenty-four hour period
But all the days of our married life

Inspiration: Valentines Day and they way I feel about it.

Angel

Sent from above one night
We connected without connecting
That jump inside that has not happened in years
At the same time the fear of rejecting

Things did not make sense
But you offered your help
I did not want to rush things
You thought I may have had wealth

I do not remember much of our time
And I doubt we will meet again
I turned from you and what was there
And what was mine, begin to mend

Inspiration: Over twenty years into my marriage and had a dream of going on a date with someone other than my wife. Woke up very happy with what I have in Patty and my relationship and did not want to go through the downside and bad parts of dating again.

Mahalo

I miss you and yet we have never met
We almost did one day
You make no bones about your presence
And I have nothing to say

You send me pictures, moving and still
Though they are not only mine
Belonging to all who care to show you attention
And desire of my affection, you display no sign

The maiden I never kissed
The woman with whom I never danced
The girlfriend I always wanted but never had
Your body I dream of close to mine yet there is no chance

You will continue to send me reminders
With what I will never share
Goodnight, my dear, as the moon kisses you now
It will never be said that I did not care

Inspiration: Never going to Hawaii.

Meet Me Where I Am

I just hung up the phone
At work standing next to my desk
I was just told we lost our baby
Being a planner, I always know the next step but this time, there was no next

I could not leave, I had to stay
At the same time I could not breathe
I could not speak of the life that was no longer with us
So different were her and my needs

In time scripture verses were spit at me
Words that carried more pain than encouragement
How can you go through what I went through and say that
Even told, "at least I have four other children",
        Is the space where their heart is open for rent?

A word of advice for those comforting the brokenhearted
It is not a time to show off your biblical knowledge
Also do not convince them of the blessings of their life
How, in reality, this is a privilege

Hold their hand, sit silently or cry with them
Be with them in their time of need when there is nothing left
If you want to be like the example Jesus set for us
When Lazarus died, he did not preach or pontificate, he just wept.

Inspiration: After our miscarriage, in our devastated state, we were
preached to and told some of the most heartless things. It was meant to
help us out of our pain but that is not always the right thing. Instead of
others not wanting me to feel bad so they try and pull me up, it is just
better to come down in my hole and cry with me. I was much more
ready to stand after my friends did that with me. These feelings flowed
into words made much easier by the song penned by The Goo Goo
Dolls, "Notbroken".

Lunch

I was speaking with another believer one day
Speaking of heaven and forever
We down here have no clue of the riches above
Yet it is fun to think of a world where pain's existence is never

I was telling her of my lunch plans the day I arrive there
And who would be at the table with me
My wife's father who I have never met and Rich Mullins
Along with Jesus, I really cannot wait to see

Attempting to not dominate the conversation
I turned the question to her, wanting to know her answer
She smiled for a second and thought for another
Ready to reveal the names that in her head were dancing

She mentioned her grandfather with whom she was close
Along with Jesus and herself, there is one more that she missed
And it was at this point that she became quiet
Emotion overcame when she thought of the final name on her list

It was her sister's baby, she said through the tears
Surmising a miscarriage, I offered my condolences
She said it was not a natural termination but a chosen one
And her sibling did not yet know her heart's consequences

I hugged and shared this valley with her
We were meant to walk through these together
I left the discussion a changed person that day
Realizing how different all of our ideas are about forever

Inspiration: Nothing is thinly veiled here as this was a real
conversation with a friend one day. Still affects me to this day.

Found

I was a little behind when we were first introduced by my wife
She had spoken so highly of you
After some time, I knew the reasons for her affection
As we quickly became more acquainted, my desire to know grew

Countless facets and personalities
There was not one emotion missed
I looked forward to our weekly meetings
The crowd grew as smaller became the list

It was so much fun talking about what you offered
Always trying to figure out what you meant
You wanted to tell, you wanted our attention
The letter was written but never sent

You let us know long before when you would say goodbye
We did not want to listen
You prepared us for your departure years before you left
In my heart, I had no idea what I would be missing

We prepared for your departure that May evening
Food and drink present, family and friends came to the airport to say goodbye
So touched we were by what you had shown us
That evening, I do not think any of us had a dry eye

You have been gone for years
We all know you are in a better place
And though cliché, I would rather have known you and now be without
Than to have never kissed your face

Good thoughts and discussions about you now
You still had so much left uncovered
And your memory is strongest when I hear your voice
Life and death uncover emotions from this lover

Inspiration: Tribute to one of my most favorite shows ever, LOST.

Winning

I am told I have everything I need
But that apple looks so inviting
My continued struggles can be solved in one visit
It could solve all my problems, it is there for the biting

I know I can handle the privilege
So many fell by the side
I have a firm foundation set in You
It would only be a righteous and holy ride

I dream of how it would taste
Everything about it would be perfect
The outcome of it's blessings would be spread throughout
Mine would be the success story, a family not wrecked

I only have visions of making things better
You would see and be so proud
Tell me anything else you want me to say
Let me taste that fruit, I want to be the one from the crowd

Inspiration: I put in a dollar for the multimillion dollar
lottery at work and then began thinking about winning
and wanting to win and as I was thinking about it, I felt
just like what I think Adam felt like many moons ago.

Thinking of You

The day ahead looks rough
An uphill grind before the sun rises
I have my bible and a shower
Ready to do battle for my little prizes

I prepare the way I need to
Not a weakness in the armor
This man is complete and ready to win
The day will end with not less but more

I then hear your memory and I smile
Immediately this soldier is disarmed
Images of us on a blanket in the spring
Vulnerability overflowing, no thought of being harmed

Thoughts of you ready me more than any regiment
Your presence makes me better all the time
I will always have you close, whether you are or not
The sun just broke the through and I am warm,
        but not just from it's shine

Inspiration: Thinking of Patty while beginning my day
at work. The thought of being just in the same house as
she is has brought me through the day so many times I
have lost count.

Pretty Liar

She said goodbye and tossed her hair
Today will be the last
Empty and without
The image she once portrayed was never cast

Waif like and her own
She now belonged elsewhere
Alone when one should not be
So few that showed her care

My hearts breaks for you because of your existence
The circumstances in your life have been impossible
I know what has happened has had to affect you
Yet you still smile, laugh, and are civil

Goodbye for now I wish you best
I am sad at your presence and absence
Your ship sails away at dusk
I pray God give you everything that was lacking
      from your parents

Inspiration: Someone our family once knew that had
an impossible home life growing up and the day she
left only to never see her again. Thinking of her.

Fill Me Up

He had it all
Money, popularity, and the hair
I was not even forgotten
One has to be known for that care

He mocked my musical favorites
His were safe and canned
Mine were drugged, angry, and intelligent
Drummer's dead, need a new one for the band

He went to the big state college
Borrowed money he did not need
I was kicked out at the local school
Education was learning how to bleed

His safety zone grew smaller over the years
A situation contrary to a career in law
Mine never existed, so I had no problem
For the first time since I breathed, embraced were my flaws

Today he lives in fear, nothing is staying the same
Terror grows in his every waking moment
I am free without expectations of mine or his
Enjoying not knowing and tomorrow's scent

Inspiration: While I was in high school I was talking with someone about how much I liked "The Clash". This person laughed, put down my statement, and then told me how good some very "safe" and actually silly bands were. He was older, intelligent, good looking, and was what every kid wanted to be going into college. As life unfolded, his world become smaller, less controllable, and his rapid acceleration of fear amazed even me. Today he is paralyzed by the unknown and the thought of death, he is not even living. In high school I was the clueless one, my how times have changed.

Still Need Help

The line was long and it was cold
I was not alone one way, in another, I was
I listened to those around me in wonderment
Food and drink riddled about, sameness is a must

Racial statement about Michael Jackson
Laughing about his death
Inconsideration for those already present
Through the flurries I can see my breath

Vocal dissatisfaction for the success of another
Prices out of this world
Decibel level set from harm to destroy
The banner of "Christian Concert" unfurled

Inspiration: The unfortunate "humanness" that surrounds us even at such a wonderful event as Winterjam, a Christian concert of multiple artists. Such actions I witnessed contradictory to the one who the concert was to glorify by those attending.

Rox

Shining within
Never to be seen
To large for any finger
And her it will always belong
Because she is the queen

Among many friends
Never being alone
But not with the same stature
Does the company it keeps
Releasing to be shown

A virgin to a miner's tool
Happy within it's home
But thinking of its brothers
Not within any longer
Is it better not being known?

Inspiration: Thinking about God's beautiful creation of the diamond.

Turn The Page

I finally get it
It is not about now
So much work put into what will erode away
Not enough into the fields where we sow

It is difficult to let go of this life
Tis the only one I will have
Releasing these clay dreams
Realizing another's is the healing salve

What is to be was never that much
Nothing compares to what we do not know
Give it all up for someone else
Deeper does the river now flow

This revelation will change the direction
Less I, me, mine and more of you
And you is not singular but plural, my friend
More than just a beautiful few

Inspiration: The perfect storm of reading "The Shack",
my oldest child going to college, signing life insurance
policies on Patty and myself, and my parents eroding
health resulted in these words flowing out. Thinking
about how on earth things that seemed important: houses,
savings, and cars really are not important…and
relationships really are.

My Little Animal

Fun and laughing which is the way it is usually with you
Smart, quick, humorous, and fun
Being your father becomes more delightful every day
And my protection of you is going to make your suitors run

You amaze me at what you bring to the table
It is so different having a girl
I have only been surrounded by testosterone
Now I am in a whole different world

Your presence brings a breath of fresh air
I never know what to expect from you
Being together is an unmatched joy
The clouds move and a beautiful day shines through

Inspiration: My daughter, who was nine years old at the time, heard the song "Animal"
by the band Neon Trees. She really liked the song but wondered why parents would
name their son Neon. Hearing this song on the radio brings me back to the times when it
is just she and I. I love my children and I love having not only a daughter but this
particular daughter.

Song of Patty

No word could make reference
Could show even a drop of my oceans of love for you
The inferno created in me sears
My skin with your every glance
The passion of love that has bloomed
Is too much for me to even wish for the future
Never before has my heart been so alive
Such a furnace fueled by just the sound of your name
My thoughts are nothing but a flow of love for you
You have awoken true love in every part of me
And never again shall it sleep
To kiss your mouth overfills any wanton of passion
That dwells within me
The rage of love that is rooted in my every pore
Will take lifetimes, no, generations to cool after ours is over
I have not yet become conscious after tasting and experiencing
Your love for me

Inspiration: Written for Patty when we were engaged and still does not do her presence
in my life any justice.

Together

Her smile at odd moments
Expressions only her own
Humor occasionally used as a guard
To disguise the true feelings not shown

I love her deeply, my true friend
A patient and loving pearl
I attempt to convey my feelings for her
Only ending in grammatical peril

What is in my heart, she will never know
So deep, pulsating, and burning
I believe that is what true love to be
Because forever my heart will be yearning

Inspiration: Written a little over two months after my dating Patty and though I consciously did not know the future, reading this poem now, it appears subconsciously I did.

Walk On

I cannot believe we lost
We need to stay in the top twenty-five
In the blowouts, I will get some minutes
A game on ESPN would be nice

I am so proud of my son today
He is pursuing his dream
Though he will never have a shoe contract
To see him in uniform on that bench, I beam

"A plane went down, a walk-on did not survive
After their loss in Colorado today
Families are being notified", university officials report
The beginning of their loss starts this way

Inspiration: Taken straight from the sports headlines about a plane crash killing a number of players from a college basketball team. I attempted to personify it from the player's point of view then his father's.

Elise

You go as far as you can go
But never a step further
Oftentimes you do not even venture that far
We have different definitions of what it means to serve

It is really all about you
How everything affects your life
You offer your insight on mine and others
And how ours increases your strife

I am still wondering if it is genetic
Because no one else I know is like this
Not really an intelligent communicator of your feelings
Resulting in less hits and more misses

If I am still asked to be a part of the brigade
Then I will accept His appointed place for me
Sometimes I will smile and nod at your unintended musings
And others, will make you open your eyes to really see

Inspiration: I once knew someone with whom there was no
exchange in communication but only her communicating
her thoughts and opinions. I oftentimes just listened but
occasionally she had to be corrected and where she stepped
too far. That usually resulted in her having problems with
me after that.

The Whangdoodle

You do not breathe fire
No, too harsh for you
The gentlest of all
But never in a zoo
You have been seen
By the innocent and young
Lost in imagination
To you, their hearts had clung
Not resembling anyone else
Though having the head of a moose
You wanted her attractive
Being King, this queen you will choose
The help of the children
With guidance of dreams
You lived endlessly and happily
With the queen
I do not believe
The you have been seen these days
But imagination is your kingdom
And there you may always play

Inspiration: A friend gave me the children's book,
"Last of the Great Whangdoodles" written by Julie
Andrews, yes, Mary Poppins, and I really liked it.
This is a tribute to the book.

Free Me

To totally surrender my life to You
Is what I want to do
To open my heart and accept your love
To become completely renewed

Shed this skin that I have been wearing
It smells, is heavy, and uncomfortable
I want to run freely in the sunshine
And be recognized by your label

I cannot change my old life to new
I can barely change my mind
But You can reach down and mold me again
Without anything to bind

Release me from the world
May my spirit fly with You
Your love is all I need in this life
Grace to heaven is to America red, white and blue

Inspiration: Learning real freedom is in Christ and
the joy of not having to please anyone on
earth...also, learning that He is already pleased with
me just because He made me, for no other reason.

Spring Dusk in Milford, OH

There are over a half dozen children in front of me
The cul-de-sac is the stadium for dodge ball
There are under a half dozen children behind me
The trampoline, their only way to be tall

The late spring dusk sky
Just too beautiful to turn away
I sigh while looking and listen to the laughing
This slice of heaven was revealed today

A major league contest being broadcast over the airwaves
Bases and balls are the soundtrack of this moment
Reminiscing my spring evenings of nearly half a century ago
Life experienced at that time, not even a thought of being a parent

Responsibilities bring me back to the present
Laundry, a wet basement, and messy kitchen calls my name
But I will answer the urge when my past beckons
And we can share this spring evening that out of nowhere came

Inspiration: All that is written is very much how this happened.

Gym

We go there to become strong
But in multiple areas, not overlapping
He needs to work on this, I need to work on that
Financially, physically, and time sapping

Few words are exchanged with many
Few exchange many words
Building muscles, egos, and friendships
In that order by the masses preferred

One man leads his woman, he should have her by her hair
Another man, bodyguarding his wife
The worst of us displayed so clearly
Is this how we are living our life

But there is a sweetness that also accompanies
A kind greeting or gesture shared
And all other silliness is washed away
Together, we will try and make it through, we will care

Inspiration: Going to the gym multiple times a week brings about many observations. These
are just a few.

Color

The silvery lake was a welcome sight
Sounds so smooth, made me feel like all was well
Christmastime this year was going to be special
As my heart was the first to tell

Harmony within and without
The grey skies, appropriate and expected
Waving goodnight to a chosen few
It would not be for years on which
      this moment was reflected

My son bouncing at home
Cinematic ties to this time
Minutes taken to express the words
Sharing and releasing what is only mine

Thank you for visiting
My mood is altered due to you
I hold my children more lovingly
Appreciation of His gift including the G cleft is not new

Inspiration: Words just flowed out upon hearing the
Coldplay song "Life In Technicolor ii". Final verse
is my tipping my hat to the wonderful gift of music.

Lights

I still miss you after all these years
Sobriety is now my constant companion
Looking out the window and it begins to snow
Emotional distance resembling the Grand Canyon

Own my house and my problems
Did it all for you
Set up the tree and hung half the ornaments
Elvis is telling me about his Christmas of blue

Getting ready for church
So glad it is only down the street
Your unopened gift sits lonely again this holiday
No new television specials to meet

Wearing mom's homemade scarf
Thinking about getting a pet
Neighbor's friends and family beginning to arrive
I yell "goodbye" to the inside of my empty home
        Another year regarded as "not yet"

Inspiration: Thinking about someone putting their
life back together after hurting those they love most
dear at the proverbial happiest time of the year.

What He Said

I was asked to be in a wedding
A "new friend" to the groom
Of all he had to choose from, I was honored
For the relationship to grow, there was room

A hot day, the picture taking was difficult
Aside without any, just sit back and watch
Asked by none for my assistance
Aligning with the guests this emotional patch

The groom and his friend not connecting for years
But tonight they are like the boys of old
Giggling, singing, and playing
For a moment the future has been put on hold

Then in a moment only between them
The friend calls the groom over in a discreet way
He speaks to him in a way where only the groom would understand
It is lengthy and completes them, more than words were said

The ceremony is holy
The reception, giving from a collection of hearts
The honeymoon, finances suggest another time
This groomsmen walks away blessed from this evening to be a part

Inspiration: Not much hidden here. I was asked to be in a
wedding and was very happy to be a part of the evening. One of
the most touching moments was when a friend of many years of
the groom called him over and spoke to him in a one way
conversation that left both men visibly moved upon its completion.
No idea what was said, but made me think about the things that
these events bring up in us and the things we say at those times of
deepest emotions.

You Are The Gift

In life I have been given many things
Some with an incredible price
Rings, cars, a place to live
All have been suffice

Then the non-tangibles enter the picture
Love, education, wisdom
Some earned, some given
To me, they have all come

What I receive in you has never been seen
Be me, ever before
So many facets in one human being
All from a beautiful love

A flower so beautiful
Never seen by this eye
When others gaze upon you
With whom does she accompany, proudly, it is I

A fourteen carat heart
Pulsating with love
You give your all to everyone
This is His gift to you from above

So lovingly affectionate
I do not tell you how much I enjoy this trait
Always touching, caressing, feeling
It is His true love that you create

The love you give so freely
No one has given me ever
I have to thank you for this gift
When do I wish to be without, never

Never before have I received such a gem
You fill the want of every pore
But as quick as you came, as soon you can go
So I promise, I will never ask for more

What I am attempting to say, Patricia
You are the greatest gift I have ever received
The life I give to Him is one hundred times better
Because it is in your love that I believe

Inspiration: Written for my wife on sweetest day.

The Edge

You blew me away at the moment of darkness
So moved and transported I was
For a moment I forgot my companion
And on a date, what a boyfriend does

Awakened was my spirit
Life is more than pizza and football games
All of a sudden I moved past so many
My existence has taken a different aim

She fell by the wayside
Theater and control called her name
Growth for knowledge called mine
And I no longer knew anyone's path with mine, was the same

I still visit every few years
Not many share my affinity for you
But I cannot tell of my change without your part of the story
And how this person became anew

Inspiration: I saw Bill Murray's film "The Razor's Edge" in
1984 with a date. The film, I feel, was a tool in God
awakening me spiritually as it eventually led to me searching
and becoming born again a few months later. I loved what it
did for me so much, I told everyone I know to see it. I was
shocked by no one really liking it...it is a very heavy film and
is about the lead character finding himself. It fit my life
accurately at that time.

Walt

The magical world opened before we arrived
Greeters to ensure safe passage
A trolley through lands before delivering
Loud and clear was the message

Visiting nations within a few yards of each other
Invention and innovation the theme
Forget automobiles, space travel is on tap
The lid taken off imagination is seems

Viewing the creatures of the earth in safety
Though our expedition to Everest appeared to put us at risk
Heat emanating from every concrete slab
Made liquid refreshment and Kali's rapids do the trick

Vaunted ceilings in a haunted hotel
Or a rolling and rocking ride
Made the day of cinema live forever
While a water spectacular provided a fantasmic night

Volumes of us walk main street U.S.A. to the castle
Memories return of Sunday night events
All our dreams come true in this enchanted world
Even in my marriage, being here makes me feel like a prince

When we arrive back home we are back to reality
Responsibilities, work, and bills await
Yet I can still escape in my mind to the fantasy resort
The reality of my visit better than any fiction an author could create

Inspiration: A tribute to my family's visit to Disneyworld.

Mine

My car has more holes in it than Dunkin Doughnuts
When it was new, I do not know but am sure it was fine
I have been teased now because of it's look
No cash for this clunker, but it is mine

My house needs so much work
And I have neither the money nor the time
Holes in the roof and a front porch missing some planks
It is not a money pit because I do not have any money, but it is mine

Mates with as many holes in their character as my car
Not anyone that will receive a presidential invite to dine
Sometimes I wish they would make different decisions
Others have rejected them, but they are friends of mine

She was probably pretty once
On her, daddy's love did shine
After the kids and her hard life, today you may not look twice at her
But I chose her then and would again, I am thrilled that she is mine

I do not have much by your standards
By all aspects I am below everyone's "success" line
This is what I drive, where I live, my friends, and who I love
It's ok they are tossed out by others, it was the only way to make them mine

The Father says "he has not done what the churchgoers have done
His tithing less in dollars and more in dimes
The world cast him aside, heck, the devil barely wants him
Yet he is my beautiful creation and I proudly and fiercely claim him as mine"

Inspiration: I thought of the guy who is happy, content with his life
though it is not a life desired by the world.

Johnnie and The Moondogs

You sang to me when I moved
Four happy heads on a plate of red
I tried to learn yours but fell short
Later you reminded me of what she said, she said

You accompanied me through my parade of suitors
The constant you provided before I met the big guy
As He entered you let him drive your car
Still being more present than just a day in my life

Fast forward from yesterday to today
When I was given your instrument of choice
Rekindling the passion that lead to teaching myself
Now all I need is the voice

You are part of the soundtrack of my life
Jesus inspired the thought of all that is needed is love
I will smile as I remember the melodies given to you
With different words, I would not be surprised by
        angels singing these tunes above

Inspiration: My multiple decade long love affair with
the fab four.

CMA

What we know is eroding before us
What should be, is not anymore
What about offending, let us not do that
What, who, where, and when is ignored

Focus is now blurred
Our map has expanded beyond our reach
Courage replaced by correctness
Tolerance, the new class to teach

Doing what is right is not the mantra
Everybody is right to some degree
Do not violate the rights of those who violated rights
Right has replaced fight, and righteousness replaced by me

I want to love some things of this earth
Yet you remind me of your words in times like these
This is not our home, very clear by what is happening
And good we see here, it is actually from heaven,
    just a tease

Inspiration: The shock I felt about the verdict in the
Casey Anthony trial and my looking to Him to make
things right…and it will not be here on earth.

Caylee

My heart hurts at the thought of you
I do but do not want to know about your last moments
I pray, like Stephen, He took you home before your last breath
Mercy for a little two, almost three, little girl sent

An angel sent to cover the four corners on Hope Springs Drive
Blessings extended and received for many months
It was not your choice to leave, but another made that choice for you
Joy now gone and hope no longer springing on so many fronts

Now the four corners have that millstone attached
Sorrow, unhappiness, and despair now very much alive
Where do they turn, where go they go
Those four corners on Hope Springs Drive

Your short mission is in some way complete
Memories of you still touch many others to move
Fostered and adopted, a new commitment is made
Hugging our own and saying no a little less, showing love

You are now held by your Father and have the
        biggest Winnie collection around
I promise to play with you and introduce my children to you, little Caylee
You will recognize us by our prayers as you do the others you are meeting
There will be a long line, but we will wait patiently

May God bless you, little one
He has in so many ways
You were a part of His mission and that is now done
Laughing and loving and never out of His gaze

Inspiration: Written for Caylee Marie Anthony.

Two Years

What was grey now has color
My heart now beats
The silvery shadows are now my friends
Yet it is impossible to meet

I remember you from your friend's party
You did not know who I was to you
We danced and kissed, your friend did not like that
Forever, chronologically speaking, was just a year, times two

You brought life into my life and yet you are so far
You are in my yesterdays, todays, and tomorrows
You write on paper, it goes straight to my soul
You ended the emptiness that accompanies my sorrow

I will wait for you, a lifetime if need be
Just to taste your lips again and hold you close
I rely on my memory of our future meeting
Not crossing the street today, anticipation grows

Inspiration: One of my favorite films, "The Lake House".

Again

Was it ten years ago or ten minutes ago
The emotion as fresh in both instances
Shock, amazement, speechlessness, tears
A day that erased political, racial, and religious fences

Every other telecast reveals something I did not know
I learn even from the ones I had seen before
Collective pain shared individually
And when we cannot take another heartache, there is so much more

This day will never be easy
The amount of victims and memories are too many
I have stopped asking why, no answer will make sense
Nowhere is the feeling of forgiveness at seven times seventy

The calendar page turns and it is a new day
Work and chores at home cloud my plans
Yesterday is not forgotten but today, it is not my focus
My emotions not in another's hands

Inspiration: The tenth anniversary of September 11th, 2001.

FB

I know what I want to do
Others think they do
No one will have more friends
Yet by then we will be half of two

Did not fit in with the others
As my plan will unify all
Alone but unifying millions
Humble beginnings in that room in a hall

We lost each other on our ride
This was not expected to happen
Pulled in different directions, we parted ways
Technology called my name while business
        on your shoulder was tapping

I now have the biggest egg and what everyone wants
But I need more of what everyone has in their nest
She said goodbye at our hello
And in the end, I just want her to accept my request

Inspiration: Was really moved at the end of the movie
"The Social Network" and was not sure why. The film
was smart, snappy, funny, sad, interesting, informative,
even though a bit embellished. I think, in the end, the
friendship ending due to a program that links friends
was so ironic, it touched me.

Look The Other Way

I try but I cannot be him
Nothing I do will make you accept me
I want to be the person you want
Through other's eyes I wish I could see

Soon my façade is taking shape
You looked once, even twice my way
I will continue to build this structure
For acceptance, it is all I will pay

You have now bought into what I am selling
I now dine and rub elbows with you
The plates are spinning on numerous sticks
This would be ok if I did not have to juggle, too

While you are looking at my illusion I go back to me
I glance her way for a smile
The only one who I was myself around
And still she treated me as vile

Inspiration: Saw a character on a show go to painful
lengths to be accepted. When he finally had the
group's acceptance, he went back to the only one
who he was not fake to yet she still treated him badly.

Needs

Dear Father
Uncertainty is the canvas while fear and terror, the palatte
Where and what am I to do next
So many issues need to be addressed.

I do not know what tomorrow brings
I am so used to your answer of "No"
I have not been short changed of blessing
But one thing I am surely not is a prophet.

Why did you put five lives in my lap?
I can not even lead my own
I heart bursts for them all, constantly training myself to love them more
While learning them and forgetting me.

Forgive me for my aimlessness, for I am of little, if any, use to you
I have wanted you all my life, and I loved our moments
It is in these multidirectional intersections that I
        have been arriving at more often
That I feel the lowest.

Bless my children with every spiritual blessing
Give Patty her heart's desire
Please give me a life with you
May I dive deep in your ocean and know nothing but you

I have found nothing that compares to a moment with you in this world
You have confirmed that in your word
May I lean only on you and your breath through the saints
For that is the food that this starving body needs.

Inspiration: Feeling unworthy of the monumental responsibility of
fatherhood and realization that the only chance of success is completely
Him.

Rachel

I have tried to write this a half dozen times by now
And I never find the end result acceptable
How can I put into words my feelings for you
Thinking of your face, smile, personality,
        I just am not able

You have no idea what an answer to
        unknown prayer you are for me
I pray God gives you the same gift
To cherish someone as much I do you
Is something I would never want you to miss

What pains my heart is you are growing older
By the end of these words, time will have passed
I can never have enough moments with you
While some unshared seconds amass

My heart leapt the day I found out I
        would receive my only girl
A smile through my tears, I showed
The feeling I had that day was just a sliver of joy
        I would feel throughout your life
While experiencing being a father to a daughter
        and the love that flows

Inspiration: My baby girl!

My Elmo

We had the group
The girls and the guys
Some dated some did not
But it was the beginning of many highs

We stood with and for each other
Yet still checked our look in the mirror
Late teens and early twenties was a good time in the skin
A blemish on date night was our biggest fear

Opposite sex friends sometimes with benefits
A cigarette was often the answer
Some would swim with us, some would not
Some would leave nothing to chance

We did not go to Georgetown but to Sycamore and U.C.
We did not have Hoolihans but McDonalds and Bennigans
Rob and Demi were not there but Scott E and Lisa H were
The hearts under their Hollywood looks beat ones of true friends

Inspiration: Watching "St. Elmo's Fire" and reflecting who my group was at that
time of my life.

Zombie

The wound was healed long ago
Today the scar is barely visible
To have a heart removed and never supported
Are conditions not for the livable

I have continued without and throughout
Not all organs are necessary
Numb can be a feeling too
There is less baggage to be carried

I do not share the emotions of others
They have and when they do not they mourn
I do not and will not as the days confirm
I wonder where it is that I have been born

Inspiration: Reflecting on my deepest hurt and the road after.

Rochelle

We worked next to each other
Helping those without
But it was we who were lacking
And learning what this walk was about

The first to meet
And the last to see each other
Bookends to a very odd foursome
In conclusion, closer than a brother

Brother Joe and Father Cal as our guides
"Did you make your board upon waking?"
A late night card fight
And a daytime fixture accompanied our faking

But what changed me for a lifetime was your willing to be there
One early morning during my loneliness
Nothing would tear you away from my story
Never before was there an audience to my mess

Your unconditional care altered my life
I have moved on actually feeling some worth
Life fit me well that next day
And you returned to your home up North

Though that moon rose and set over two decades ago
It still feels as if you just unlocked my chain and released
I will never forget that mile you walked with me
And now others, I have helped out of their prisons, pain has ceased

Inspiration: Written for my friend Greg Gamble from New Rochelle, New
York. Greg and I were on a mission assignment in the summer of 1987. I
was going through a pivotal moment in my walk with Christ and felt
completely isolated. He made himself available to listen, really listen, which
is something I had not experienced from a friend before. Through Greg,
God guided my back to communion with Him. Though you will never read
this, thank you, Greg, for being there for me that July evening into morning.

NFD

Pure is the way you live
You know no other way
Joy in activity at all times
Restriction is a word you will not even say

All is good in what you see
You do not wear glasses that are rose colored
They are rose colored retinas
And a refreshing way to see the world

I occasionally become frustrated with you
Wanting you to understand the way I do
This is this and that is that
If I raise my voice maybe that rose will become blue

Then the big guy steps in and corrects me
"Jack, he has my view of reality, one I once gave you
Ask for me to give you my eyes and you will see like Noah does
Let's get back to that rose and away from the cold blue"

Inspiration: My son Noah has the most pure view of the world
and because he does not think like me at times, he frustrates
the life out of me….but upon further inspection, his view is
actually one more spiritual, and one that I need to have more
often. Thank for the reminder, Noah, I love you and love the
way God created you. Forgive me for the times I did not see
you the way He did and my continual prayer is for Him to give
me His eyes for you, and your brothers and sister.

Hello?

I am dancing
Saying, "hey look at me"
Doing all I can for the attention
Yet in my nightmare no one can see

Feeling I am doing what I am called
You just smile
Working for the end result
Your distance from me, over miles

Will power diminishing
Why do what I do for this
The filament in this bulb is fading
If not recognized, it cannot be missed

A sad forever slumber in the thicket
The foliage does enough to cover
This body exhales one last time
Darkness consumes externally and internally another

Inspiration: Thinking about how one would feel
who thinks they have nothing left to live for.

Above

It is getting dark as I walk home
Externally, so far, internally so near
The dark purple sky suggest it's cold precipitation
My desires, too strong to give in to the growing fear

I do not recognize the dwellings on my journey
Though they are brief in this trial
Keep going and soon we will be
Unknown to me are the traveled and
     yet to be traveled miles

Remembering my youth on this walk
I had it really good
Mom and Dad made a glowing home for us and ours
If I am given such a day, the same I would

To disappear within the unknown
Festivities will carry on without me
I am at peace and it is ok
One less Christmas ornament hung on the tree

Inspiration: Thinking about the beginning of that
instant of twilight in the walk from life to death.

Fourth, Yet First

Princess, I have begun this poem more times than you know,
Trying to capture into words being your daddy
      has been more difficult than I first believed;
But the effort of attempting to write it, to you, this I owe,
It is the least I can do, and cannot be compared
      to what you have done for me.

I remember I cried the moment I found out you were a girl,
Much like the time when you found out Joshua was a boy,
      though for different reasons;
I finally had my daughter and that would never become plural,
I had been waiting for you for many seasons.

You have been such a gift to me and God
      could not have given me a more beautiful flower,
I do realize and appreciate what He had done for me through you;
The thought of you makes me smile and your approach
      to life makes me laugh,
You have not been out manned in this family,
      in fact they had better watch out for you.

I do not dream about your wedding, though I know
      Mr. Brightside will be there,
Nor do I think about your children, though ten is
      a big number to ignore;
I think about the times we have shared for they have been
      so rich, I feel almost unfairly blessed,
So I look forward to our next hug, laugh, wrestle, and dance,
      for you are my princess, how could I ask for more?

Inspiration: My fourth child, but first daughter.

Joe's Field

It opens on a foggy night
Green grass below
The dew collects on my shoes
Clueless, yet I still know

The word home just multiplied to me
My heart has never been more full
All I can imagine and much I could not
Has confirmed my belief in a soul

So many roads actually intersect
How can one keep track of so much
His walk, her age, my life, their death
The almighty existing is truth and no longer a crutch

My game, my girls, my dad, my home
Past hall of famers now my brethren
I look at all before me as I conclude
Even if this is Iowa, it is my heaven

Inspiration: Putting myself into the mindset of the
lead character, Ray Kinsella, from the book
"Shoeless Joe" by W.P. Kinsella and the movie
"Field of Dreams" which is one of my favorite.

Closure

The healing has begun
The light green wafty grass now grows where char existed
The pond a bit more full after the drought
Where the boo-boo was, mommy has now kissed

A faint scar where the life changing wound was present
The corners of a smile where a scowl dwelled
That bit of warmth in that cool early spring breeze
Noticing softness while still laying where I fell

That first sip of cold water after that immeasurable thirst
The smell of the feast after that lengthy fast
Sight after the scales fall away from my eyes
Turning my head forward, deciding not to focus on the past

Being made whole is a gift from above
Especially after certain death was looming
My gardener wants me to have faith as completeness
    was always His plan
Never was the pain for no reason but a necessary and
    rewarding pruning

Inspiration: After a very difficult situation with
someone, grace, mercy and forgiveness were initiated
on both sides to make things whole again.

To Sir With Love

The first summer night where it was not scalding
A nice drive to the river
Singing in anticipation with my son
Just to see him, the evening will have delivered

Sitting, talking, and watching was the warm up
Excitement brighter as the lights dimmed
Young and old held each other
No hope of change but of yesterday brimmed

You said hello in your own way
We all loved your language
You sang as did we as there was never an awkward silence
All we needed tonight is love was your pledge

Tears welled about all your loving
I loved the new firemen song
Your wingspan was much larger than we all imagined
And the encore was so much shorter for us than long

My son and I drove home that night
He had a glimpse into the window of my teenage soul
A fragmented relationship, for moment healed
A son seeing his father as a boy left a vision for full

Inspiration: My son and I seeing Paul McCartney in August of
2011 at Great American Ballpark. One of the best and most
anticipated concerts of my life…about thirty years.

Know

For the first time I see what the flower has to offer
A bird's existence amazes me
Foliage and growth never witnessed before
The clouds alone are a reason to be

I do not need to move to be a part of this
But I do have to stop
Ceasing is allowing my beginning
As I harvest this living crop

To become one, words cannot express
Floating towards what is the plan
Without my eyes, I see differently
No longer is there sea or land

To each his own
Though another does not breathe
All is clear and no question remains
The doors are for entering not leaving

To suggest a fifth dimension would be limiting
Explosions of the senses is weak
To know all and be with He who is
Finally, never ever needing to seek

Inspiration: These are the words that flowed when hearing
Thomas Bergersen's incredible melody "Remember Me".